A Poet's Primer

A Guide to Classic Forms

By
Jack Huber

Books by Jack Huber available at JackHuber.com:

Aspects Long Forgotten
A Splendid Alternative
A Troupe In Masquerade
Trappings of the Years
An Eerie Calm Before the Night

The author welcomes comments via email. Send messages to jack@jackhuber.com.

First Edition, September 2010

Table of Contents

Preface 5

Notations and Definitions 7

Poetic Meter...10

Poetic Forms..14

    Abhanga 14

    Acrostic..17

    Balassi Stanza 19

    Blitz..21

    Chōka...25

    Cleave 27

    Clerihew 29

    Crapsey Cinquain....................................30

    Diamante..32

    Diminished Hexaverse.............................34

    Dizain...36

    Epulaeryu 38

    Etheree 39

    Fibonacci 41

    Haiku and Senryu 43

    Kyrielle..45

    Lento 47

    Monchielle...49

    Musette 50

    Ode 52

    Ottava Rima...54

Pantoum 57

Pleiades 60

Prose and Free Verse 61

Puente 64

Quatern 65

Quintana 68

Rictameter 71

Rimas Dissolutas 73

Rondeau 75

Roundelay 77

Ruba'i 80

Septolet 82

Sestina 84

Sijo 88

Sonnet 89

Standard Habbie 92

Tanka 95

Terza Rima 97

Trilinea 99

Triolet 100

Villanelle 102

Virelai 105

Wave Poem 107

Epilogue 109

About the Author 111

Preface

With rap, slam poetry and prose so popular these days, I set out to learn and master many of the oldest poetic forms that have been evolved through the centuries, some developed in or before the Middle Ages. I learned some newer forms as well, and created my own format.

Forms can be based on a wide variety of patterns (or non-patterns), such as stanza and line counts, syllable counts, meter, rhyming scheme, theme and a "turn" or poignant finish. The familiar haiku format of five, then seven, then five syllables in its three lines transcends meter and rhyme. It requires a theme of nature or the seasons and may include a "cutting word," which cuts the stream of thought during reading for any one of a variety of purposes. An English sonnet, on the other hand, is fourteen lines, typically in three quatrains (four-line stanzas) and a couplet (two-line stanza), which uses classic meter and a strict rhyming pattern. A sonnet sometimes employs an unexpected turn, called a "volta," that may change the feel or even the theme of the poem, and the final couplet often serves to sum up the subject or purpose of the poem in two lines.

One can only master these forms by employing them, both with successes and failures guiding the education process. I'll steal a quote often used by Robert Keim, the inventor of the blitz poem. He intimates that poet Theodore Roethke once said, "Sometimes an apparent constraint can serve to free the imagination." To be confined by a stringent format forces a writer to think outside of their normal vocabulary, past cliché or colloquialism, and in so doing, may find passion or poignancy where it may otherwise have been lacking. Often the difficulty is in employing a format that guides the reader to your point without their noticing, that flows from the lips without struggle and in the case of rhyming work, that they are as natural in speech as any conversation would be. If you accomplish these things with your poem, you have indeed mastered the form.

My readers, students, friends and family who follow my poetry often ask, "You know so many forms, how do you choose one?" My answer is always, "It depends." Truthfully, form, meter and rhyme schemes all play a part in the feel of a poem.

Sometimes I decide I haven't written with a certain form for a while, or need to create an example for an article. I am an "ekphrastic" poet, meaning I derive inspiration from a visual art, namely my photographs, so I might start by looking through my photos to find something whose inspiration somewhat matches the feel of the form on which I've pre-decided.

Sometimes it's the opposite- I am already inspired and look through the various formats at my fingertips until, hopefully, I find the form that most closely fits.

Occasionally that means looking up new forms I've yet to try, though that number is shrinking. If I have a lot to say, or am telling a story, I'm not going to select haiku, a sijo or another very short form. If it is serious or deep, I might not want to pick a limerick style or Dr. Seuss-like rhyming format. Even so, I might start with one form and discard it for another part-way through.

In this primer I will describe over forty formats and I'll try to bring a little history or explanation to them when I'm able. I will also include examples of each, nearly all of which will have come from my own hand.

Notations and Definitions

Throughout this book I'll be using different types of notations for specific guidelines.

Syllable
A syllable is the most basic unit in a word and is usually counted by vowel sounds, even if not physically included in the written word or separated by consonants. For example, "cat" is one syllable, "bottle" is two syllables, "avenue" is three, "incandescent" is four, "mitochondria" is five and "evolutionary" is six syllables. A dictionary is the best source of the number and pronunciation of syllables in a word.

An important aspect of a syllable is whether it is stressed. This can be difficult to grasp, but a stressed syllable has more force while speaking than unstressed syllables. Some may call this an accented syllable. In the word, "aspect," the stressed syllable is "AS-" and unstressed is "pect." In "discuss," the stressed and unstressed swap places- "dis-CUSS."

Foot
A "foot" is a combination of stressed and unstressed syllables and is the smallest repeating pattern in a line. These are the building blocks of the lines in poetry and upon which "meter" depends.

Meter
Meter is the pattern of syllables used in poetry, including the arrangement of stressed and unstressed syllables in each line, and the sequences that are used in multiple lines. For notation's sake, I use a dash for unstressed syllables (-) and a carat for emphasized ones (^). So, "- ^ -" means, " dah-DUM-dah," like "consider" or "in fashion."

The number of syllables in a line can also be very important. You'll find a complete discussion in the chapter, "Poetic Meter."

Stanza
A stanza is a grouping of lines with a break, or blank line, before the following stanza begins. This is the poetic equivalent of a verse in a song.

Refrain
A refrain is a word, phrase or line that is repeated one or more times in a poem.

Rhyme
Simply, a rhyme is the sharing of an ending sound between words in two or more lines. Some aspects of rhyming are described by the terms "perfect," "imperfect," "assonance" or "half-rhymes." There are many other types of rhyming, but these are the four primary uses. Perfect rhymes are, as you would expect, straightforward matching of ending vowel and consonant sounds, such as "bite" and "might," or "ball" and "wall". Imperfect rhymes are otherwise perfect in rhyme but the rhyming syllables are stressed differently, like "king" and "purring". Half rhymes just rhyme consonant sounds, not vowels, such as "tall" and "will".

There are contemporary styles that use assonance instead of perfect rhyme, which means rhyming only vowel sounds ("make" and "bait", or "kite" and "bike"). Besides pure laziness, this has become especially popular because of lyrics. In music, both meter and rhyme can be loose because the singer can adjust syllables to be as short or long as the beat and rhythm allow, and the music itself lessens the audience's attention to the details of rhyming.

Use of assonance in rap is the norm and rather plentiful, which is also true of some "slam poetry".

In rhyming pattern notation, the alphabet is used to designate the rhyme partnerships. For instance, lines ending in a sound designated by "a" only rhyme with other "a" lines, "b" lines only with other "b" lines, and so on. A great example is the Spenserian sonnet, which uses a rhyming scheme of:

a-b-a-b ... b-c-b-c ... c-d-c-d ... e-e

The " ... " designates a stanza break, but blank spaces may be used ("a-a-b b-b-c"). In the example, line 1 rhymes with line 3 (the "a" lines); line 2 rhymes with lines 4, 5 and 7 (the "b" lines"; line 6 rhymes with 8, 9 and 11 (the "c" lines); and so on.

The line, "they have seen the policeman's holster" would have the notation, "- - ^ - - ^ - ^ -". Written another way, where emphasized syllables are capitalized, it would be, "they have SEEN the poLICEman's HOLster." The abbreviated notation, though, is more effective in comparing lines and is what I recommend.

You may come across some forms that dictate masculine or feminine rhymes. As a rule, I discount their importance to a format, but their proper use in rhyming can be effective. A rhyme is considered masculine if only one syllable matches, usually at the end of a line, such as "chart" and "part," or "confusion" and "commotion." A feminine rhyme matches two or more syllables, like "painted" and "acquainted," or "fashion" and "passion." Most often the last matching syllable in a feminine rhyme is unstressed.

Poetic Meter

Meter is the pattern of syllables used in poetry, including the number, stressed, and unstressed syllables in each line, and the patterns that are used in multiple lines. A "foot" is the smallest repeating pattern in a line, so five feet of " - ^ " (called an iambic foot) would look like this:

_ ^ _ ^ _ ^ _ ^ _ ^

Example:

"the pitch will soon be coming to the plate"

Five iambic feet is called "iambic pentameter" and is a meter I use often. Just four iambic feet in a line is called "iambic tetrameter", and you can trade off within stanzas, making odd lines pentameter and even lines tetrameter, for example.

It is also acceptable to vary by a syllable if it makes the poem smoother to read, or is necessary in projecting emotion, but I strive for perfect meter, taking it as a personal challenge.

Just remember that once you start a meter pattern, you must keep that pattern throughout, unless a particular form requires a change. There are forms, such as haiku, that are meter independent, so maintaining a meter is not only difficult, but undesirable.

Interestingly, some of the best unrhymed poetry uses meter for rhythm and flow.

As I mentioned, the simplest and smallest repeating pattern of meter is called a "foot" and the number and kind of feet make up the meter in a line. I wrote about iambic pentameter, one of the oldest classic meters and quite often used in sonnets, including five iambs (or iambic feet of "dah-DUM").

Of course, we're talking about patterns of syllables. Simply, a syllable is a basic unit of speech generally containing only one vowel sound. The word "basic" contains two syllables [ba-sic]. The word "generally" contains four [gen-er-al-ly]. This means you'll need to count vowel sounds, not vowels. "Table" has two vowel sounds, as does "people" and "capture." "Advertisement" has four syllables; "deanthropomorphization" has eight [de-an-thro-po-mor-phi-za-tion].

Most often trouble in determining syllables is with local speech or dialect. While I had always taken for granted that "orange" was two syllables, sure enough I came across someone who pronounces it "oinj." A few more examples: "prayer" can be pronounced "pray-er" or "prare;" "wandering" can be "wan-der-ing" or "wan-dring;" "wheel" might be "we-ull" or "wele;" "world" is pronounced both as "wurr-uld" and "whurld." There are many more of these; a poet must take care in helping the reader, if possible, to pronounce a word the way he or she intends. This is done with context, placement in a line and obvious meter pattern. If pronunciation of a word might distract from a poem, sometimes I'll toss the word and use something else, even if it means completely rewriting a line or stanza. Knowing your audience can really help with these decisions.

The simplest way to ascertain where syllable breaks are and which are stressed in a word is to look the word up in a dictionary, such as dictionary.com. For example, the captions for the word "aspect" might be "**as**-pekt" or "as' pekt". Both show the syllable breaks and that "as" should be stressed (bold on the first and an apostrophe on the latter). Using a word in a sentence can change the stress of one or more syllables, so the dictionary reference is only a guide.

The following are the most common types of meter:

• iamb – one unstressed syllable followed by a stressed syllable (- ^)
• trochee – one stressed syllable followed by an unstressed syllable (^ -)
• dactyl – one stressed syllable followed by two unstressed syllables (^ - -)
• anapest – two unstressed syllables followed by one stressed syllable (- - ^)
• spondee – two stressed syllables together (^ ^)

The number of metrical feet in a line are as follows:

• dimeter – two feet
• trimeter – three feet
• tetrameter – four feet
• pentameter – five feet
• hexameter – six feet
• heptameter – seven feet
• octameter – eight feet

I'll sometimes write in anapestic trimeter or tetrameter, such as:

I will travel the world in a month (- - ^ - - ^ - - ^)
Please remember your manners when visiting Ted
(- - ^ - - ^ - - ^ - - ^)

When choosing a meter, you can mix patterns, usually in alternating lines, but remember that, normally, you should keep that combined pattern throughout the poem. You can also add or subtract a syllable at the beginning or end of an otherwise classic metrical line as long as you are consistent, or it enhances the flow or emotion of the poem. In other words, it's okay to purposely break the rules once you know them. Shakespeare often added and subtracted syllables from his patterns.

Financial debacle was fast on our heels,
> (- ^ - - ^ - - ^ - - ^ = anapestic tetrameter minus the first syllable)
we managed to stay just ahead
> (- ^ - - ^ - - ^ = anapestic trimeter minus the first syllable)
by moving to Kansas and Midwest ideals,
> (anapestic tetrameter minus the first syllable)
a shelter from cash flow in red...
> (anapestic trimeter minus the first syllable)

The most important aspect of meter is consistency and flow. When in doubt, write down the pattern notations for your whole poem and the inconsistencies will usually be obvious.

Poetic Forms

Abhanga

The "Abhanga" (or "Abhang") originated in India in the seventeenth century as religious discourse or devotional poetry. They were first written and sung by those considered saints, such as a popular poet of the time, Tukaram. Numbering in the 5,000's, to this day abhangs are sung in ritual marches by devotees of Indian saint-poets Namdeo, Tukaram and Dyaneshwar.

Because of their small size and simple rhyming scheme, contemporary poets, both Indian and others, have begun using the form in non-religious writings. Simple abhanga are four lines in length, with respective syllable counts of 6, 6, 6 and 4. In addition, the middle two lines rhyme while the outer two do not. Thus, the rhyming scheme is "a-b-b-c."

Typical variations include multiple stanzas and different rhyming schemes. For one modified abhanga, included below as an example, I wrote it in a series and made the four-syllable last line of each stanza a refrain. Other poets have even dropped the rhyming scheme altogether, making it similar to haiku or tanka.   As with most poetic forms, there is no naming convention, so the title is of the poet's choosing.

Examples:

Lucy

Lucy's ears are straight back
when she's let loose to run,
her legs a blur, now done-
she's out of breath.

A "Wizard of Oz" Cairn,
but with a coarse blonde coat,
she whines a piercing note
with snacks about.

The North Wind Blows

When chill of winter comes
amidst the autumn air,
with months ahead to bear,
the north wind blows.

The lake, abandoned, both
by fools and wiser men
they spurn the open when
the north wind blows.

The climate's cold decline
has yet to be complete,
with snow about to greet,
the north wind blows.

Devoid of human touch,
abyss derides the shore,
and always, as before,
the north wind blows.

Now winter does emerge,
a blizzard in mid-course,
with horizontal force,
the north wind blows.

The roads and towns are closed
for dangers of the cold,
as storms of ice unfold,
the north wind blows.

A lessening occurs,
a warming trend remains,
still everyone complains,
the north wind blows.

Once spring has come at last,
it's soon to be outdone,
yes, even in the sun,
the north wind blows.

Acrostic

An acrostic is a poem inside which a word, phrase or message is imbedded, typically using the first or last letters, syllables or words in its lines. It can be used in other writing devices as well, such as acronyms for names of organizations (i.e. laser- Light Amplification by Stimulated Emission of Radiation) or memory aids (such as Roy G. Biv- Red, Orange, Yellow, Green, Blue, Indigo, Violet).

In poetry, an acrostic regularly utilizes the first letter in each line to form a word that the poem describes (or vice versa). However, there are many patterns available to the poet.

A double acrostic may use the first letters of lines for one word or message and the last letters of the same lines for a second word or message. The two may or may not be related.

These all assume that the author wants to be obvious in its message. There are also ways to disguise an acrostic, i.e. placing letters, syllables or words in the middle of lines, or placing them on every other line. For example, the Dutch national anthem is an acrostic using the first letter of each of fifteen stanzas, spelling out WILLEM VAN NASSOV (another name for William of Orange).

An acrostic may or may not employ meter or rhyme. There are no guidelines as to number or length of lines or stanzas, and though some poets title their work using the "hidden" message, that is not a requirement.

Example:

An Acrostic (by Edgar Allen Poe)

Elizabeth it is in vain you say
"**L**ove not" — thou sayest it in so sweet a way:
In vain those words from thee or L.E.L.
Zantippe's talents had enforced so well:
Ah! if that language from thy heart arise,
Breath it less gently forth — and veil thine eyes.
Endymion, recollect, when Luna tried
To cure his love — was cured of all beside —
His follie — pride — and passion — for he died.

Balassi Stanza

Balint Balassi was a 16th century Renaissance lyricist who was the founder of modern Hungarian poetry and, interestingly, was the first author of Hungarian erotic poetry. His most well-known poetry involved his love of Anna Losonczi, whom was married but seemed to respond to his attention. After the death of her first husband, she remarried and his love for her went unrequited. Balassi enshrined her in verse when his pursuit of her failed.

In developing his form, Balassi took an existing format of three 19-syllable lines and split each line into thirds, adding recurring rhymes, to make stanzas of nine lines. The number of syllables in each line of the stanza still totals 57: 6-6-7-6-6-7-6-6-7. Like many syllable-based poetry, there is no set meter required.

Balassi became known as using far better and more original rhymes in Hungarian than any other poet before him. His primary rhyming scheme was:

a – a – b – c – c – b – d – d – b

Though many examples are single verses, there can be any number of Balassi stanzas in a poem. Balassi himself used many variations of his format in his religious poetry and in his erotic poems, and many contemporary poets have followed suit.

Example:

Fisherman's Task

How many times, I ask,
was a fisherman's task
to clean the catch of the day
upon this lakeside dock
by barely four o'clock,
well before the skies turned gray?
The handle of the pump
would jitter, clack and thump,
to wash that night's fish buffet.

Blitz

The "Blitz" poem is well-named, as fifty short lines are read in rapid-fire fashion. This form was invented by poet Robert Keim in 2008. I traded correspondence with Mr. Keim, who is a 10th grade English teacher in upstate New York. It seems that he has a class poetry project for his students that involves thinking outside of the box. His "poetry portfolio project" is extensive and includes both writing and interpreting poetry.

In describing his teaching goals, Mr. Keim quotes Theodore Roethke, "Sometimes an apparent constraint can serve to free the imagination." In this light, classic and new poetic forms play significant roles in his teaching, and allow greater creativity in student writings.

Always on the lookout for fun and interesting ways to introduce poetic forms to his teen students, he came across a word association game on-line, which started the gears moving in his mind. His classes were too large to utilize the game directly, but the word association process brought out a great mixture of cliché's and well-known phrases. Though clichés are usually frowned upon in poetry, a form based on them would be fun and different, and allow poets to somewhat disguise their intentions or message.

Explains Mr. Keim, "I wanted to have something that, while being a form poem, sounded free and wild. I really like the irony that a poem that is free-association has rigid rules. Poetry is often about such juxtapositions, and a well done form poem flows despite the 'rigidity' of form."

He decided on a long blast of short phrases, and on a length that could be "read at a frantic pace to the point of nearing exhaustion (as the name 'blitz' implies), which also lent itself to ending the poem with single word lines for a fade-out effect, hoping that the last two words would leave a lasting impression."

The format is unique- twenty-four couplets, each line beginning with the last word of the previous couplet, ending with two single word lines, the last word of lines 48 and 47, respectively. As mentioned, the lines are short and fast, but consist of at least two words (other than the last two lines), and most are cliché, common or recognizable phrases. The blitz lends itself well to being read aloud.

There is no meter or rhyme used in a blitz. Though fast-paced, the concept that the poet wants to convey will be revealed slowly throughout the piece, as less meaningful phrases give way to those more relevant when taken in total. Continuous repetition through the poem keeps the reader (or listener) interested and allows for a quick cadence. The ending tends to be a poignant comment on the concept delivered.

At first glance, it appears to be an easy form to use, but upon embarking, you'll find it challenging. The first line is a short phrase, perhaps a cliché, and the second line repeats the first word of the first one. The last word of line two is the first word of lines three and four, the last word of line four is the first word of lines five and six, and so on until the last two lines. Line 49 is simply the last word of line 48, and line 50 is the last word of line 47.

The title should be exactly three words, joining the first word of line 3 with the word in line 47 with a conjunction or preposition. Mr. Keim says he "purposefully selected the guidelines for title... in an effort to create a quasi-recursive/enveloping effect for the reader/listener." He also intended to give the writer a sense of direction, particularly if the title was selected before the poem was written.

Example:

<u>Country May Fly</u>

Mother nature
mother country
country 'tis of thee
country road
road apples
road leading home
home to roost
home at three
three white birds
three dog night
night owls
night vision
vision of paradise
vision of the future
future probabilities
future is now
now and forever
now we can see
see how they fail
see to it tomorrow
tomorrow never knows
tomorrow isn't soon enough
enough waste
enough time has past
past experience
past tense
tense muscles
tense times

times like these
times are changing
changing doctrines
changing minds
minds will follow
minds made up
up the canyon walls
up in the air
air your dirty laundry
air raid
raid the environment
raid the piggy bank
bank on it
bank of the great river
river of waste
river runs wild
wild oats
wild and fancy free
free to fly
free as birds
birds...
fly...

Chōka

Another of ancient Japan's many poetic forms, chōka may be the longest of them. Chōka may be translated as "long poem," the opposite of tanka ("short poem"). In fact, chōka guidelines dictate a minimum length of seven lines, but no maximum.

Like haiku, senryu and tanka, chōka does not rhyme and has specific syllable counts in each line. The most basic chōka has three couplets with syllable counts of five and seven per line, plus a last seven-syllable line. This format allows a lengthy poem, using as many 5-7 couplets as the author chooses, then the finishing line. Thus, a nine-line chōka would have the following syllable pattern:

5 – 7 – 5 – 7 – 5 – 7 – 5 – 7 – 7

Like the other Japanese forms, titles of chōka may be taken from the poem's first line, or a key line, or may simply be numbered, though naming poems is completely up to the author without specific rules.

Example:

Camouflaged

Suitably quiet,
he succeeds in blending in,
quite invisible,
while he waxes nonchalant.
Indeed, he'd rather be
anything but recognized,
just another sapling
camouflaged by the forest.
Every now and then

he is freed from his cocoon
and shows brilliantly
his talent for spectacle,
as crippling stage fright
releases its hold on him
ever so slightly.
Whispers become raucous songs,
telling the world, "Look at me!"

Cleave

There is a movement afoot, a grass roots evolution to promote a relatively new poetic form, the cleave. I found literally dozens of cleave websites, all of which are chock-full of posted submissions. The cleave was invented by Dr. Phuoc-Tan Diep, an admitted "Vietnamese boat person, a refugee in England." His drive to describe his life of dichotomy fueled his design of this very unusual format.

The cleave is three poems in one. There is a vertical left half (the left side of each line is read vertically top to bottom), a vertical right half (top to bottom on the right), and in total. Writing a cleave can be complex, as you might imagine. Each segment must fit in all three poems; the left and right poems should be able to stand on their own as good poetry, and the fusion of the two should lead to an insight that enhances the individual halves.

There are no guidelines as to number or length of lines, and meter and rhyme is discouraged. Often either the left or the right half is shown in bold to assist the reader in discerning the halves. When reading the full horizontal poem, it should be read as if the separation didn't exist.

Examples:

The Lonely Blossom

A single blossom in field of grass, - a yellow floret protrudes,
out of place in this pasture, - lonely in a sea of green,
calls out to passers-by, - and hopes for friendly visits,
honey bees and hummingbirds - to help with propagation,
trade pollen with distant blooms - with staid anticipation.
It struggles amidst the cattle - this flower tackles a tenuous life,
afraid of the inevitable - roots holding on dearly,
until it happens - a bovine hoof, unaware,
the weakened stem severed - a flower's foolish hopes,
along with its yellow petals - crushed..

<u>Judging Without Knowing</u>

It's the same every night - **my dreams betray me**
a new spot, new faces, new music - **thrusting me in the spotlight amid**
their probing eyes - **this troupe with thespian masks**
I'm the stranger in their midst - **judging without knowing**
Someday I may fit in - **though I wear chagrin on my sleeve**
I hope, while I take my turn - **I will show myself worthy to be**
in the unending rotation - **on this raised platform**
I'm not unknowable - **and shall be accepted after all.**

Clerihew

A clerihew is a humorous 4-line poem about a celebrity, named in the first line. Often the celebrity's name comprises the entire first line. Invented by poet Edmund Clerihew Bentley, a Clerihew pokes fun at someone famous or puts them in an absurd light, though is not abusive. It is common for a Clerihew to parody short eulogies.

There is no set meter. In fact, the Clerihew usually contains irregular line lengths. The rhyming scheme of "a-a-b-b" can be comically contrived.

The title of a Clerihew is always the name of its subject.

Examples:

Charlie Sheen

The great Charlie Sheen
is a fan of caffeine,
especially when his head is tender-
recovering from his latest bender.

Tom Hanks

Tom Hanks
must own some banks.
He's almost Donald Trump
in the guise of Forrest Gump.

Crapsey Cinquain

A cinquain can refer to any five-line poem with a set pattern or syllable count. Adelaide Crapsey, however, made the cinquain her own. Born in Brooklyn, NY, in 1878, at the turn of the century she was class poet at Vassar College in Poughkeepsie. Before her death of tuberculosis, her interest in haiku and tanka led her to develop her own cinquain patterns, as well as a new form of the "doublet," a couplet that utilized two rhyming lines of ten syllables each. Much of Adelaide's work was published posthumously and it was Carl Sandburg's poem, "Adelaide Crapsey," that re-established her and her art form in popular culture.

Without rhyming, the Crapsey cinquain was most often written in iambic meter ("duh-DUM") and had a set syllable pattern. Its 22 syllables were arranged in lines of 2,4,6,8 and 2 syllables, respectively, for lines one through five.

Crapsey cinquains are the most popular but variations do exist. A "reverse cinquain" has a syllable pattern of 2-8-6-4-2 and a "mirror cinquain" pairs the Crapsey or standard cinquain with the reverse. Combining the two "mirror cinquain" stanzas and eliminating one of the two-syllable lines in the middle creates a nine-line "butterfly cinquain." Link five stanzas and you have a "crown cinquain." There seems to be no shortage of variations.

Titles are at the poet's discretion.

Examples:

Lightning

Its flash,
a brilliant test
of nighttime's secrecy,
exposes for an instant, then
escapes.

Cardinal

Red bird,
your glorious
plumage is radiant,
as your male ego is displayed
for her.

Diamante

The diamante, or diamond poem, was created by Iris Tiedt in 1969. It is a diamond shape when center-justified and follows strict rules, line by line. Because of its dependence on adjectives, strict form, and lack of meter and rhyme, many elementary school students are taught this form as an entry into poetry and creative writing.

The diamante is a single stanza made up of seven lines. The top and bottom lines are single words, nouns, and the poem converges between them at the center line. These two endpoints should be synonyms or antonyms (such as friend/companion or love/hate), and all the words and phrases in the lines between them will be describing one or the other.

Rules governing the diamante:

Line 1: noun
Line 2: two adjectives describing the first noun (L1)
Line 3: three adjectives that describe the first noun (L1), all ending in "ing"
Line 4: four words- two regarding the first noun (L1), two regarding the synonym/antonym (L7)
Line 5: three adjectives that describe the synonym/antonym (L7), all ending in "ing"
Line 6: two adjectives describing the synonym/antonym (L7)
Line 7: synonym/antonym of the first noun

I have found no guidelines for naming a diamante, so it is the author's choice, but it seems natural to use the first line as the title.

Examples:

Sculptures

Sculptures
rowdy, whimsical
amusing, engaging, inviting
exotic, outrageous, provocative, eccentric
compelling, alluring, riveting
imaginative, inspired
Art

Freedom

Freedom
earned, coveted
perservering, redeeming, uplifting
liberty, emancipation, ascent, eminence
rising, towering, overlooking
heightened, exalted
elevation

Diminished Hexaverse

One would think that a poetic form with the name "hexaverse" would have stanzas or lines or syllables equaling six, such as in "hexagonal," or six-sided. However I found no strict definition of a hexaverse anywhere on the usual Internet search engines or even on the two dozen or so poetry sites I researched. "Hexaverse" is currently underlined in red in my Microsoft Word page as a misspelled word, though I know it's spelled correctly. It seems like the hexaverse gets no respect.

Most of the poems I found online that represented themselves as "diminished hexaverse" start out with a five-line stanza of five syllables in each line, then a four-line stanza with four syllables each, and so on, until the last one syllable stanza ends the poem. The reducing line and syllable count is why the form is referred to as "diminished."

The one site I found that actually defines "diminished hexaverse" mentions that five need not be the starting line and syllable count. If this is the case, I now pronounce that the obvious should be true. From this day forward a diminished hexaverse should indeed start out with a stanza of six six-syllable lines, followed by a stanza of five five-syllable lines, then one of four four-syllable lines, etc.

One variation I would propose would be an "increasing hexaverse," which would be the reverse of the diminished version, starting with one syllable and increasing lines and syllables in each stanza until culminating with a six-line stanza with six-syllable lines. Another variation would be to increase the base number, i.e. start with ten lines of ten syllables each, and so on.

As with most syllable-based forms, rhyme and meter are to be avoided. There is no titling convention, so one may name their hexaverse anything they like.

Example:

The Majesty of Sunset

No one could prepare me
for the resplendency,
the esteemed majesty,
of the mid-March sunset,
in which the falling sun
drapes itself in such red.

So unexpected!
I've seen the sun set
on the horizon
for ten thousand eves-
but not like this one.

Crimson doesn't
do justice to
these hues of deep,
darkening skies.

Reverence
is evoked,
though short-lived.

Watching,
I'm in
awe.

Dizain

The Dizain has its roots in 14th and 15th century French poetry; details of its earliest use are difficult to gather, but the time frame seems to correspond to early sonnets, as poets sometimes chose between the two forms.

The dizain is a complete poem containing only one verse ten lines, or sometimes eight, each using eight or ten-syllables, and rhyming in a specific pattern. If it has ten lines, it may also be called a "decastich." The number of syllables should be the same for every line, either eight syllables or ten. There should be no variation from line to line.

Although there is no specific meter required in a dizain, it is customary to use a classic meter, such as iambic pentameter (see the "Poetic Meter" chapter).

Using only four rhymes, the rhyming pattern should be:

for the original ten-line stanza-

a – b – a – b – b – c – c – d – c – d

and for the octet, or eight-line version-

a – b – a – b – c – d – c – d

Naming is at the poet's discretion.

Examples:

A Masterpiece Revealed

He gently leapt from frond to lanky stem,
while dragging with him bonds of future meals.
With expert stitching, strands became a hem,
completing this, his latest of ordeals,
and only when the morning dew reveals
this masterpiece can others grasp his skill.
He'll lie in wait, quite patiently, until
a passerby flies blindly in the space
reserved for those whose protein fits the bill,
then wrapped, preserved in unrelenting lace.

Frenchie Finds a Friend

When Frenchie met the hefty dinosaur,
he hoped the beast was not a fan of frog,
instead he wanted friendship, a rapport,
for loneliness had settled like a fog,
still missing Pete and Moss from his old bog.
He'd never seen a dinosaur 'til now
so mustered all the courage he'd allow,
a mighty leap, up to its line of sight,
revealed a friendly gaze below its brow.
The creature smiled, much to the frog's delight.

Epulaeryu

The Epulaeryu is a short poem that describes or features culinary delights. Author Joseph Spence, who invented and named the form, put the Latin word "Epulae," translated "feast," with an Asian term, "Ryu," which means "form" or "style." Accordingly, "Epulaeryu" would come to mean a poem about a feast or other culinary art with which the poet is especially fond.

The form typically describes various courses of a feast or meal, and ends in a singular interjection and an exclamation point, portraying the author's excitement in the cuisine and its presentation. From the description in total, the reader should have a good sense (and taste) of the main course.

The Epulaeryu is a seven line poem consisting of thirty-three syllables, arranged in the following manner: 7-5-7-5-5-3-1 and "!" (seven syllables in line 1, five in line 2, and so on).

As with many other short forms, there is no rhyme or meter. The title is at the poet's discretion.

Example:

¡Ole!

Guacamole on warm chips,
spicy Spanish rice
and refried pintos served hot,
corn shucks discarded
to reveal piquant
tamales,
¡Oh!

Etheree

The poetic form, "etheree," uses syllable count rather than meter and is unrhymed. The basic form has ten lines, the first consisting of exactly one syllable, the second line of two syllables, and so on until the last line's ten syllables. An etheree can also be reversed, starting with ten syllables and ending with one.

A "double etheree" combines the two, so is twenty lines, starting with one syllable, counting up to ten. Line eleven also has ten syllables and each line thereafter reduces by one.

Examples of the Double Etheree:

Once

Once,
I drove
past a house,
haggard, exposed
to the sun and rain,
decaying roof and steps
warding off all passers-by.
I looked past the abandoned shack
to an era of prosperity,
envisioning a house, a family.

Once, this battered relic was freshly built,
occupied and enjoyed, an abode
with children's ruckus clamoring
through its carpeted hallways,
grandparents arriving
for evening supper,
taking turns on
the porch swing,
at home,
once.

Looking Over Your Shoulder

Work
can seep
into your
personal life,
friends and confidants
caution; you have to keep
looking over your shoulder.
Jealous co-workers are watching,
waiting for private indiscretions
to prove they, not you, deserve advancement.

They can't compete with your intelligence
or experience, so they conspire
to find your hidden skeletons.
Looking over your shoulder
can be a tiresome chore,
distracting you from
more important
concerns, with
little
gained.

Fibonacci (aka Fib Poetry)

The Fib, or Fibonacci poetry, is based upon a numerical sequence named for a twelfth century mathematician, Leonardo Fibonacci. Though Fibonacci did not invent the sequence, he made it popular in his book, "Liber Abaci" ("Book of Abacus" or "Book of Calculation"), published in 1202. The sequence begins with 0 and 1, and each subsequent number in the sequence is the sum of the previous two. Thus, the first few members of the list are 0, 1, 1, 2, 3, 5, 8, 13, 21, 34, 55, 89 and so on. For example, to figure the next number in the sequence after 5, you would add 5 and the previous number, 3, to get 8. Then, 8 and 5 is the next number, 13.

Poets throughout history have utilized interesting sequences in their poetic forms, and for centuries they have used the Fibonacci sequence as a guide for haiku-like poems. The numeric values typically represent either the number of syllables or words and usually is limited to just the first six members of the sequence beginning with 1.

Like the mathematician Fibonacci, who made the sequence well-known but was not its inventor, poet and screenwriter Gregory K. Pincus again made the "Fib" popular in 2006 by posting in his blog an explanation and an invitation to his blog fans to write and post them online. The Fib was briefly a web phenomenon and even today there are several websites dedicated to it.

As mentioned, the each line in a Fibonacci poem corresponds to its place in the Fibonacci sequence (without counting the initial 0), the quantity of which determines the number of syllables or words in that line. Most Fibs, however, are just six lines and utilize syllable counts, in the succession 1, 1, 2, 3, 5, 8. Like most syllable-based formats, there are no rhyme or meter requirements, and no naming convention.

Examples:

Spring Orchid

Wild,
spring
orchid,
eccentric
in its choice of bed,
seems content in its arrangement.

Before the Mast

Sail,
wind,
planning,
first dogwatch,
then, before the mast,
we let ourselves be cast away.

Haiku and Senryu

Haiku is one of the oldest Japanese forms of poetry. Originally written about the seasons of the year, currently nature is also an acceptable theme. Since haiku and senryu are such widely studied and described forms, I'll forgo the history lesson.

Haiku does not rhyme and consists of 17 syllables in three lines in a 5–7–5 format (five syllables in line one, seven in line two, then five again). In classic haiku, there is usually a "cutting word" that turns the thoughts of the reader in an unexpected, sometimes ironic, direction.

Although "haiku" has become a catch phrase that includes any and all 5-7-5-formatted poems, there are other forms with that format. Senryu can be thought of as haiku that features human foibles or characteristics of life rather than nature or the seasons.

There is a contemporary practice, to which I do not subscribe, of labeling any short poem that utilizes the traditional haiku themes and cutting words as haiku. In my opinion, this is a slippery slope. Already I have seen "haiku" of 4-3-4 or 4-6-4 format about a myriad of subjects other than the seasons. I like the constraint that traditional haiku rules provides.

Since they are short, titles of haiku or senryu often are taken from the poem's first line or are simply numbered, though naming poems is completely up to the author without specific rules.

Examples:

Spring Harvest (Haiku)

Spring harvest begins
when revealed petals call out
for tiny visits.

Autumn Prepares Trees (Haiku)

Autumn prepares trees
for the brutal cold coming-
a sleeping forest.

Intensity (Senryu)

Loud explosions fuel
the thrill of intensity
in a stuntman's heart.

Footprints (Senryu)

For one brief moment
the world can tell I was here,
then sands recover.

Kyrielle

The kyrielle has its roots in the Middle Ages, when troubadours sang madrigals and wrote kyrielle poetry. Once popular in Christian hymns, these often contained the refrain, "Lord, have mercy."

The kyrielle is written in couplets (two-line stanzas) or quatrains (four-line stanzas) rhyming in couplets, with a minimum of three quatrains or six couplets. There is no set maximum of stanzas.

Strictly speaking, each line consists of exactly eight syllables and the last line of each stanza is a refrain. A refrain is a line that is repeated one or more times in a poem. Variations include iambic pentameter (five feet of "dah-DUM"), or other classic meters (see the "Poetic Meter" chapter).

Common rhyming schemes include:

a – a – b – refrain(b) ... c – c - b – refrain(b) ... z – z - b – refrain(b)

or

a – b – a – refrain(b) ... c – b - c – refrain(b) ... z – b - z – refrain(b)

"Refrain(b)" is the repeating line that rhymes with other "b" lines.

Examples:

This Quaint Facade

Though quietly I spend my time,
a dozen decades past my prime,
I feel the years of life's debris-
I'm not the person that you see.

This quaint facade will serve its use,
no pressure to perform, produce,
a sculpture of humanity-
I'm not the person that you see.

While missing friends of childhood,
I know I wasn't understood,
emotions churn and wrestle free-
I'm not the person that you see.

Too Much Rain

Abundance is a plight today-
indulgence, thought to cure our banes,
instead can cause vast disarray,
like quenching drought with too much rain.

A widow mourns and shuns her friends,
an over-treated youth, insane,
a lonely man shoots up and spends
existence blaming too much rain.

While moderation is the key,
the need for over-kill remains
a human foible fraught with glee,
while rivers flood with too much rain.

The cure for sadness isn't born
from opulence or pink Champagne;
we can't escape the past or scorn
with turgid love or too much rain.

Lento

The lento was invented by poet Lencio Rodrigues. He explains on poetry sites that he named the form after his own first name, but rhymed it with another form, the Cento. He also mentions that the format came to him in a dream, much like many of his writing inspirations.

The lento consists of two quatrains, or four-line stanzas, that use either of the following rhyming schemes:

a-b-a-b ... c-d-c-d
a-w-a-x ... b-y-b-z

Lines ending in a sound designated by "a" only rhyme with other "a" lines, "b" lines only with other "b" lines, and so on. "w," "x," "y," and "z" do not rhyme with any other lines. Rhymes can be perfect or just similar sounds.

The interesting twist in this form is that the first word in each line rhymes with other lines in its stanza, the scheme being, "e-e-e-e ... f-f-f-f." So, a typical rhyme scheme with first and last words of each line represented might be:

e.....a
e.....b
e.....a
e.....b

f.....c
f.....d
f.....c
f.....d

Four quatrains would make a "double lento," six would make a "triple lento," and so on. There is no set naming convention, so authors may select titles as they like..

 Example:

<u>Wyoming</u>

Dwell on Wyoming, its soft, clouded sky,
smell the plains' air as the fragrances drift,
tell us of eagles in early July,
quell nature's passion before spirits lift.

Nights in the open are filled with such stars,
rites of the passage of earth and of man,
sites where a clan had drawn circles and bars,
whites and dull reds in a Yellowstone tan.

Monchielle

The Monchielle poem was developed and described by Norwegian poet Jim T. Henriksen. This form consists of four quintains (five-line stanzas) in which the first line in each stanza are refrains. All lines are six syllables in length in any meter, though usually iambic or trochaic trimeter (see the "Poetic Meter" chapter) is preferred. Lines three and five in each stanza rhyme while lines one, two and four do not.

The Monchielle's theme is not restricted, nor is its title.

Example:

Behold the Hawk

The hawk surveys the grounds
with keen and focused eyes,
no movement will escape
attention; none will taunt
this feared and stoic shape.

The hawk surveys the grounds,
his kingdom, from the trees,
majestic wings await
a mouse or smaller bird
oblivious to fate.

The hawk surveys the grounds
as afternoon declines
the ravens' calls begin
a frantic chorus line,
his brothers closing in.

The hawk surveys the grounds,
his nest and mate nearby,
well past the harvest moon,
there is no time to waste
with winter coming soon.

Musette

Besides a type of musical instrument, a French bagpipe, a leather carrying pouch or a form of French dance, "musette" can also refer to a nine-line poem consisting of a total of twenty-four syllables.

Constructed with three stanzas of three lines each, the very short lines give a poet an avenue to be poignant, much like a haiku or tanka. Its rhyming pattern can add a subtle musical quality, thus the name.

The syllabic pattern is strict: the first and third lines of each stanza are two syllables each and rhyme only with each other, and the second lines are four syllables each and do not rhyme at all. So, the rhyming pattern is:

a − b − a … c − d − c … e − f − e.

With such short lines, there is no meter. The title is at the poet's discretion.

Example:

Bemoaning Autumn

Leaves fly
on frigid wings,
limbs sigh

as wind
traipses through them,
chagrined,

for though
winter's not here,
they know.

Tines Turn

We reap
past waning light–
no sleep.

Tines turn
on the cart rake,
wheels churn

through grass,
dried hay and feed,
en masse.

Ode

The ode has been rarely used in 20th or 21st centuries, but poets now write them on occasion to accentuate a theme. Originated by the Greeks as choral songs, especially in Greek drama, odes were arranged in stanzas that included moving from a lyrical premise ("strophe"), a return to the premise ("antistrophe"), and a finish ("epode"). Interestingly, in a drama, the Greek chorus would literally walk across the stage while singing the strophe and back again while singing the antistrophe.

The ode evolved in the 19th century to become lyrical poetry rather than songs and over time has come to mean any metrical poem that has a lyrical quality. Since then, odes have directly spoken to their subjects.

Since being lyrical is at its heart, an ode should be written in a classic meter, such as iambic pentameter or tetrameter (see the "Poetic Meter" chapter), and utilize extensive rhyming patterns. There is no set stanza style or length. Though not a requirement, "Ode" is often used in the title.

Example:

Ode to the Boom Crane

What would we ever do without your towers?
A grace that stands against the cobalt sky.
your silhouette could fascinate for hours,
the height and deft of muscle you supply.

A beam of gray floats silently above me,
suspended from a ribbon made of steel,
from left to right you swing around the birch tree
and carefully your gears unwind the reel.

While each of levered arms supporting lattice
of trusses and a maze of countless walls,
without your Herculean apparatus,
there wouldn't be skyscrapers, cities, or malls.

My eyes perceive the beauty of your profile,
and like the gentle birds that share your name,
you rise above the turmoil and the junk pile,
with little thought of what the world became.

Ottava Rima

Ottava rima poetry was originated by Italian poets in the fourteenth century. They began as epic poems (extremely long, multi-stanza poetry) about heroic or religious subjects, but eventually became known for their mocking of these themes.

Probably the best-known ottava rima poems in English were written by Lord Byron, including "Beppo" in 1818, as well as "Don Juan" and "Vision of Judgment," both penned in the early 1820's. Other notable poets using this form are Percy Bysshe Shelley and William Butler Yeats. One of Yeats' most popular pieces, "Sailing to Byzantium," was ottava rima.

An ottava rima is one or more octets (8-line stanzas) with ten or eleven syllables per line. They are almost always written in iambic pentameter (see the "Poetic Meter" chapter). The rhyming pattern is similar to the sonnet and, in fact, the ottava rima was an important part of the evolution towards the sonnet. The format is:

a-b-a-b-a-b-c-c … d-e-d-e-d-e-f-f … x-y-x-y-x-y-z-z

The "x-y-z" stanza just shows that it's the last stanza in the series. There can be any number of stanzas in this form.

There are examples of variations to the ottava rima format. "Sailing to Byzantium" used half-rhymes, for example, where only the consonant or vowel sounds were repeated rather than the whole phonic sound ("with" and "wrath" or "from" and "gun"). One may also ignore using the mocking nature that was originally employed. There is no requirement for the title; it is at the author's discretion.

Examples:

Our Canine Paladin

We're sure the robbers shudder in the night
just thinking of our canine paladin,
while Lucy sniffs the air for signs of plight,
in every nook and cranny that's within
her boundaries, in case intruders might
ignore the risk of scratched or punctured skin.
Alas, we've seen the mighty Lucy hide
behind us when she hears a noise outside.

Portraying fearlessness is just a show,
for terriers project their self-esteem
for all to see, from breeding long ago,
they are the leaders of their home regime.
From safety Lucy barks to let them know
to keep this house apart from any scheme,
but with a simple knock she hits the floor
with body wags for any at the door.

Ghosts from August Herds

When wandering the backroads of the plains,
where waving grass makes way for corn and wheat,
secluded from the noise of speeding trains,
you leave behind the fractured asphalt street.
There, ghosts from august herds may yet remain,
the thunder almost felt beneath your feet
as native horsemen flush their bison prey,
and others force the herd in disarray.

An arrow in the heart, a bison spins
and promptly drops while others are pursued.
The chase complete, they load the meat and skins
to consummate their quest for warmth and food.
Tonight they celebrate, a feast begins,
and then the season's hunting will conclude.
At times the festival still breaks the hush
of evening plains among the sedge and brush.

Pantoum

Originally "pantuns" were written in ancient Malaysia. From them the French began developing the pantoum ("pan-TOOM") in the nineteenth century as a set of quatrains (4-line stanzas) which utilize refrains in a set line pattern. It may utilize a classic meter and/or rhyme, but this is not necessary in order to conform to the pantoum's guidelines. The minimum length of a pantoum is three stanzas, but there can be as many as the poet wishes.

In a pantoum, the second and fourth lines of each stanza are repeated as the first and third lines, respectively, of the following stanza. In addition, the final line of the poem is a repeat of the first line of the first stanza. Ideally, each refrain would have a different meaning from its first use, accomplished by changing context with the lines around it, or by using punctuation or punning.

Because of the many refrains that repeat from other stanzas, an interesting rhyming pattern can be developed. For example, taking "a-b-a-b" as the first stanza's rhyming scheme, and the poem's last line repeating the first line of the first stanza, you might well have the following pattern:

a-b-a-b ... b-c-b-c ... c-a-c-a

As with many classic forms, there are many variations to the pantoum. For example, some poets will repeat the third line of the first stanza as the second line in the last stanza, thereby allowing them to use every line in the poem twice.

The standard pantoum is written in the following line pattern:

L1
L2
L3
L4

L5- repeat L2
L6
L7- repeat L4
L8

L9- repeat L6
L10
L11- repeat L8
L12- repeat L1 (this is the final stanza)

Examples:

<u>The City on an Inland Sea</u>

Its downtown skyline on display,
this city on an inland sea,
it draws the ruralites away
from lonely roads and storms' debris.

This city on an inland sea,
with much to teach and lots to learn
from lonely roads and storms' debris,
it asks so little in return.

With much to teach and lots to learn,
the Chi-town's heart is open wide,
it asks so little in return
from those who share its civic pride.

The Chi-town's heart is open wide,
it draws the ruralites away
to those who share its civic pride-
its downtown skyline on display.

The Guide

Let the bluebird guide you, for she knows
the hidden direction of coming distress.
She'll wait for you, as long as it takes,
you can follow without your archaic burdens.

The hidden direction of coming distress,
it's not always evident without succor.
You can follow without your archaic burdens;
you can bolt those doors and move forward.

It's not always evident without succor,
but the maelstrom finds strength in the past.
You can bolt those doors and move forward,
let the bluebird guide you, for she knows.

Pleiades

Named for the famous star cluster, a Pleiades is a seven-line poem without any set meter or rhyme. The seven brightest stars in the constellation were named for the "Seven Sisters" in Greek mythology, thus the seven lines. This form was invented about a decade ago by Craig Tigerman, an editor for Sol Magazine, an online poetry periodical.

A Pleiades has a one-word title and each of its seven lines begins with the same letter as the first letter in the title.

Examples:

Weathermost

When the brilliant burst lights the sky,
We count off the seconds aloud,
Willing the delay longer before thunder
Wields its booming voice, interrupting our
Watch for the storm's next strike. Having
Withdrawn, our attention now returns to the
Window into Nature's electric choreography.

Grapes

Gourmands recollect each German variety, the
greens, pinks and yellows of the noblest of fruit,
gladdened when they can sip a favored vintage,
gregarious in their oenologic oratory.
Gallant stewards smile, agreeing that
Gewurztraminer indeed goes well with salmon, as
ghosts of vineyards past hide in the dry aromas.

Prose and Free Verse

Prose and free verse are very similar in nature and are often labeled together. I frequently use "prose" to describe both, which has become common literary practice. Neither uses meter or rhyme, but classic prose is less constructed and tends more towards common speech. In fact, prose may even be written in paragraph form and is regularly adopted for discussion of facts or events.

Though free verse, also called open verse, does not normally utilize meter, a "flow" is desirable, so that readers don't find themselves tripping over phrases, and its lines are often fairly equal in length. Free verse may also utilize stanzas, which may be arranged in triplets (three-line stanzas) or quatrains (four-line stanzas), for example, but, by definition, is not tied to any repeating pattern. Stanzas can make easier the reading a lengthy poem, rather than a long paragraph or unbroken list of lines. However, any stanza breaks are up to the author and not constrained by order.

Free verse is easily the most popular form in poetry today, as poets are not saddled with the constraints of structure. For this reason it is the simplest to write, but can also be the among most difficult to master. Novice poets use prose and free verse to candidly pour out their feelings, which does not always make for good reading. An accomplished poet, however, may use free verse to steer the reader to a point or to be poignant.

Examples:

<u>Shades</u> (prose)

As the sun's rays die away in the heavens, twilight emerges from the earth. Twilight: a great army of the night, with thousands of invisible columns and billions of soldiers. A mighty army that from time immemorial has contended with light, broken in rout with every dawn, conquered with every nightfall, held sway from sunset to sunrise, and in the daytime, scattered, has taken refuge in places of concealment and has waited.

--Boleslaw Prus (1847-1912)

<u>A Splendid Alternative</u> (free verse)

So rarely does a small town become
a beacon, but her initiatives have potential,
a blueprint that may shine the light
of technology on the rest of the country.

Going green wasn't their first choice,
but as a town lay in ruins, they were bold.
What was chosen was more than survival-
it was a splendid alternative.

Greensburg didn't just rebuild.
It set rules of construction that made
itself an example, a guide for the future,
a Platinum paragon.

Choices made, alternatives were clear;
history has found this quaint Kansas town.

A Hundred Years Later (free verse)

The tall gravestone, the one on the far left,
that old chap never saw the Grand Canyon,
never dipped his toe in the Pacific Ocean,
he supported his family every day of adulthood.

Just to the right, her, she saw the world,
Paris, Tel Aviv, Sydney, Barcelona, Rio,
spent her years in a truly jetsetter fashion,
dated but never married, never anyone's mom.

Just in front of those, a couple is buried
together, though they died two years apart,
she didn't finish her last thousand-piece jigsaw,
though it did keep her grief away, for a while.

Sights seen and unseen, tasks completed or not,
ways lived, means earned, goals met or forgotten,
friend of the battle-worn or conscientious objector,
these matter to no one a hundred years later.

If it weren't for my great-great-grandfather,
I wouldn't be here, or perhaps, I wouldn't be me,
but I never cared a wit about his dreams
and his day-to-day scrambles to attain them.

A hundred years from now, my own ancestors
will go about their own struggles and successes,
I can make reparations to leave them a legacy,
still, my days here and now will matter to no one.

Puente

"Puente" means "bridge" in Spanish, and the so-named poetic form is built around one. This intriguing form was invented by poet James Rasmusson and described by ShadowPoetry.com. This one especially caught my eye because I grew up in La Puente, a suburb of Los Angeles.

Constructed in three stanzas, the first and third are separate thoughts, conditions or elements, but share an equal number of lines and the center "bridge" stanza. This middle stanza is but one line and is enclosed in tildes (~) to distinguish itself as both the last line of the first stanza and the first line of the last stanza.

The meter and rhyming are at the poet's discretion, free verse being perfectly acceptable. The title is has no guidelines; it need not match the bridge stanza like the example below.

Example:

The Dilettante's Garden

The heiress dabbles in chic baroque as if
each artifact was made for her solitary
amusement, while commoners are unaware
of her ardor for her superb private grounds,

~the dilettante's garden~

required an architect's touch, its design
first penciled on a bit of used stationary,
yet rendered a horticulturalist's dream,
now a flawless, serene arboretum.

Quatern

A quatern is a sixteen line French form composed of four quatrains (4-line stanzas), but has a repeating line that changes location in each stanza. The refrain begins as Line 1 in the first stanza and drops down one line in each quatrain.

A quatern has eight syllables per line. It does not have to use a classic meter nor follow a set rhyme scheme, but may very well contain both.

L1-Refrain
L2
L3
L4

L5
L6- Refrain (L1)
L7
L8

L9
L10
L11- Refrain (L1)
L12

L13
L14
L15
L16- Refrain (L1)

There is no naming convention. Remember to select the refrain first and try to make it memorable or poignant, since it will be repeated in each stanza of the quatern.

Examples:

Sailboarder

It's me alone against the world,
that's how it seems atop the crest
of wind-pushed wave; my upright wing
is punishing my arms and chest.

There's something thrilling just to know
it's me alone against the world,
as each gust lifts at breakneck speed,
and tempests keep the whitecaps swirled.

My aching fingers start to swell,
the hours linger through the day,
it's me alone against the world,
with nature's fury on display.

I've realized exotic dreams
of surfing with my sail unfurled,
The Great Lakes beg to take my bet,
it's me alone against the world.

Subtle Clues

When nature gives you subtle clues,
it's best to not ignore her signs,
the morning sky is just a ruse
unless you read between the lines.

A hummingbird may give a wink
when nature gives you subtle clues,
to disregard the clever link
may end you up on nightly news.

The weather stations take their cues
from past experience, they know
when nature gives you subtle clues
you may survive the coming show.

The winds can blast, the snows will drift,
but shelter will prevent your blues,
you had the sense to heed the gift
when nature gave you subtle clues.

Quintana

I developed this form in 2007 when quatrains (four-line stanzas) didn't quite fit my inspiration and quintains (5-line stanzas) seemed awkward without any guidelines. I did write in sestets (six-line stanzas), and while that was somewhat satisfying, it wasn't a perfect solution. Sometimes five lines are just right. Like haiku, a line set apart from the constraints and patterns of previous lines in a stanza can accentuate a point or thought. The solution to otherwise clumsy "loose ends" was to tie them to each other.

Based on quintains, the quintana uses classic meter and a set rhyming pattern. As mentioned, what sets the quintana apart from other quintain poems is its unique handling of the last line in each stanza. Themes are not specifically set by the form, though a poignant description of the world is preferable to internalized subjects.

The fifth line of each stanza may have different poetic aspects than the first four lines, but the meter and length of fifth lines must correspond to all of the other fifth lines. There is no upper limit as to number of stanzas, but the minimum is two to insure a fifth-line pattern.

The standard rhyming pattern for a quintana is:

a-b-a-b-i ... c-d-c-d-i ... e-f-e-f-i ... g-h-g-h-i

or some variations:

a-b-a-b-i ... c-d-c-d-I ... e-f-e-f-j ... g-h-g-h-j
a-a-b-b-I ... c-c-d-d-i ... e-e-f-f-j ... g-g-h-h-j
x-a-x-a-e ... x-b-x-b-e ... x-c-x-c-e ... x-d-x-d-e
       ('x' lines do not rhyme)

Many other rhyming variations are allowed as long as there are rhyming lines and they don't conflict with quintana's guidelines. I have left naming up to the poet.

Examples:

Dormant

With harvest time now months ago
and fallen leaves long whisked away,
a grapevine seems to suffocate,
its barren limbs a sad display,
a remnant of its life before.

A passerby might mourn the loss,
remembering the green of spring.
For now concern would be misplaced
as dormancy will keep the sting
of winter from its living core.

If only humans had this lapse,
protection from these hardened times,
a dormant season sans the pain
of money, love or social crimes,
of life too tortured to ignore.

Alas, the vines know fully well
that warmth will soon awaken roots.
As slumber ends the green will find
recovered leaves and growing shoots,
a vineyard's luscious spring decor.

An Architect Speaks

If you peek at the architect's pad
you will see what a craftsman might sketch,
a small window to musings he's had
when he's given the freedom to stretch
his imagination.

You won't see the sharp squares of his youth,
the rectangular buildings that trace
kindred lines, a distortion of truth;
no, the world's not a uniform place
of delineation.

Semicircular summits extend
the sweet curvature, arching to span
a great foyer, for eyes to ascend;
he perceived it before work began-
his celebration.

Its construction is on a quick stride
for completion in four or five weeks;
it will act as the humanist's guide
to the world, for the architect speaks
with admiration.

Rictameter

There seems to be no end to syllabic-based formats. The rictameter was invented by two cousins, Jason D. Wilkins and Richard W. Lunsford, Jr., who had started their own poetry club. The "Brotherhood of the Amarantos Mystery" was inspired in 1989 by the dark but stirring movie, "Dead Poets Society," starring Robin Williams. In their weekly "Brotherhood" meetings, Jason and Richard held private poetry contests and experimented with new poetic formats, eventually coming up with the "rictameter," which Jason apparently named after Richard. Since then, the rictameter has gained in popularity, with several websites now dedicated to or highlighting this form.

The syllable counts are specific in the rictameter. A single stanza begins and ends with the same two-syllable word, and in between the syllable count rises, then falls, by two syllables per line, with line five being the center and longest line. Thus the lines have the syllable count, 2-4-6-8-10-8-6-4-2, for a total of 50 syllables.

As with most other fixed-syllable forms, there is neither meter nor rhyming required, nor is there any tenet as to subject matter. Rictameter variations do exist, such as multiple stanzas, allowing for storytelling, and relaxing the strict number of syllables required in each line by plus or minus one. One may use the repeating word for the title, but as you can see from the examples, this is not a requirement.

Examples:

Idyllic

Quiet
shouts idyllic
in this pastoral scene-
though blackbirds pierce the perfect calm
with echoed intermissions, forgiven.
Am I awake, I ask the mare
as she feeds, or am I
hungering for
quiet?

Islandish Artists

Artists
are fierce rivals,
with colorful banners
and gaudy wall hangings as their
weapons of choice, though only the tourists
suffer the crass contemplation
of the offerings from
these islandish
artists.

Rimas Dissolutas

Rimas dissolutas poetry was developed in France as an alternative to the more intrusive rhyming that classic poetry had embraced. Rather than rhyming within stanzas, this form utilizes outside rhymes, with lines in each stanza corresponding to the same line number in other stanzas.

In addition, especially in longer pieces, half- rhymes or slant rhymes lessen the impact even further by rhyming only final consonants or similar sounds.

Rimas dissolutas can be any length of any number of lines and stanzas, with the caveat that each stanza must have the same number of lines. First lines rhyme only with other first lines, second lines with other second lines, etc.

Thus a rimas dissolutas based on five-line stanzas has a rhyming pattern as follows:

a – b – c – d – e ... a – b – c – d – e ... a – b – c – d – e ...

Traditionally, this form is considered a syllabic one, meaning that each line would usually share the same number of syllables. This aspect, though, has seemingly fallen out of favor with contemporary poets.

Another variation repeats the end words in the first pair of stanzas in subsequent pairs.

Example:

The Crossing

As each car rattled, one by one,
my day dream done and patience tried,
graffiti-filled, the rusted gates
continued with no end in sight.

My boredom forced, illusion spun
the train cars in a merry ride
around my head, its packing crates
were blurred by passing cracks of light.

The clacking, like a Gatling gun,
drowned out the crossing bell beside
the intersection's warning grates
and "R R" sign of black and white.

A calm returned, my waiting done,
the last few cars remained in stride,
now free to roll past interstates
and others watching, left to right.

Rondeau

The rondeau is a form of French poetry that was a verse form commonly set to music in the 14th and 15th centuries. Now an English language form, a rondeau makes use of an interesting refrain pattern that is frequently regarded as a challenge, using the refrains to make the poem as poignant as possible.

Because of its lyrical origins, a rondeau most often uses a classic meter, like iambic tetrameter (see the "Poetic Meter" chapter).

Perhaps the best-known rondeau is the war memorial poem, "In Flanders Fields," by Canadian poet John McCrae (1872-1918).

The rondeau consists of fifteen lines, thirteen of which are typically eight syllables in length, that include two refrains. Both the refrains are the first half of the poem's first line. A refrain is a line that is repeated one or more times in a poem. There are only three rhymes and three stanzas, including the half-line refrains:

Stanza 1: a (includes refrain) – a – b – b – a

Stanza 2: a – a – b – Refrain c

Stanza 4: a – a – b – b – a – Refrain c

Often a rondeau will take its title from its repeated half-line, but this is not required.

Examples:

A Farmer's Life

A farmer's life is far from rich--
no riding crop or muzzled twitch.
He can't be cowered in debate,
his hardened life a useful trait
to spurn a stubborn sales pitch.

He tills an irrigation ditch,
steps back and throws its dampened switch.
How much the socialites would hate
a farmer's life.

With horses gathered to unhitch,
he leads them, thinking of his niche,
how nights are free to contemplate
the land and crops of his estate,
and how his loving wife bewitched
a farmer's life.

Beware the Troll

Beware the troll as he may lie
in wait for those who happen by,
this bridge is home, the woods are near,
where traces of them disappear,
and none can hear your distant cry.

His stores are down, but he will try
to swiftly augment his supply
of children's foot and puppy's ear-
beware the troll.

The afternoon may go awry
for those who watch the cloudy sky
instead of heeding, staying clear
of trestle willows weeping here,
on fables now you may rely-
beware the troll.

Roundelay

There is some confusion online as to the meaning of the term "roundelay," with some references confusing it with the French "rondelet" and others describing it as any poem with a refrain. Actually, the roundelay, rondelet, rondeau, rondel, and other similar sounding poems all spring from a common French origin, but are all very different in contemporary use. The roundelay's many repeating couplets and limited rhymes can make it a difficult form to write, but as with many successful poems with refrains, can also make for profound or esoteric poetry.

The roundelay consists of four sestets (six-line stanzas) made up of twelve repeating couplets (two-line stanzas), one of which repeats as each stanza's last two lines. The stanzas' couplets A,B,C,D ,E and R (the continuing refrain) combine in the following pattern:

A B R ... B C R ... C D R ... D E R

So, in the second stanza, "B C R" represents six-lines (three couplets), with couplet "B" repeating from the first stanza, couplet "C" repeating in the following stanza, and its last couplet "R" repeating as every stanza's last two lines. In addition, each couplet's first line rhymes with other couplets' first lines and all second lines rhyme with each other as well, making the rhyme scheme:

a-b-a-b-a-b ... a-b-a-b-a-b ... a-b-a-b-a-b ... a-b-a-b-a-b

Trochaic tetrameter (see the "Poetic Meter" chapter) is a requirement, but it is permissible for some of the lines to be one syllable short. Naming is up to the author.

Examples:

Cannons Silent

British moving ever shoreward,
ardent plans will soon be blooming.
Soldiers hunkered, never cowered,
even with the battles looming,
cannons silent, pointing eastward ,
wait to start their endless booming.

Soldiers hunkered, never cowered,
even with the battles looming,
captain's orders pass on forward,
throes of hunger, still consuming.
Cannons silent, pointing eastward ,
wait to start their endless booming.

Captain's orders pass on forward,
throes of hunger, still consuming,
painful groans, a muffled curse word,
doubts about the war's resuming,
cannons silent, pointing eastward,
wait to start their endless booming.

Painful groans, a muffled curse word,
doubts about the war's resuming,
feasting on the peppered game bird,
skillets cleaned but fires fuming,
cannons silent, pointing eastward,
wait to start their endless booming.

Red Horizon

Now that sunset has begun,
hues make ordinary grand,
I must ponder at each one,
contemplating as I stand-
red horizon's setting sun,
rising for the distant land.

I must ponder at each one,
contemplating, as I stand,
light diminished 'til there's none,
day forgotten out of hand,
red horizon's setting sun,
rising for the distant land.

Light diminished 'til there's none,
day forgotten out of hand,
what I've lost, some others won,
much as tides return the sand,
red horizon's setting sun,
rising for the distant land.

What I've lost, some others won,
much as tides return the sand,
yin and yang, the world has spun,
darkness there will now remand,
red horizon's setting sun,
rising for the distant land.

Ruba'i

"Ruba'i" is Arabic for "quatrain", and is used to describe a Persian quatrain, or its derivative form in English and other languages. Robert Frost's "stopping by Woods on a Snowy Evening" was a very popular ruba'i.

Also known as the rubaiyat, the typical English rhyming scheme is:

a-a-b-a ... b-b-c-b ... c-c-d-c ...

In a string of rubaiyat quatrains, with the non-rhyming line taking the rhyme from the following stanza, you can make it "cyclical" by using the first rhyme ("a") as the non-rhyming line of the last stanza:

a-a-b-a ... b-b-c-b ... c-c-d-c ... z-z-a-z

In Persian verse, a ruba'i is visually only two lines long, its rhyme falling at the middle and end of the lines. Though a ruba'i generally uses a classic meter, it is not a requirement.

Example:

The Vase (a cyclical ruba'i)

In hands of discipline, a stern
reminder of his painful skill,
his fingers stiffen, knuckles burn,
as muddy clay begins to turn.

The ceramista from Brazil
exerts a steady pressure still,
a vision slowly taking shape,
projecting his artistic will.

The potter lets the time escape
while choosing tools to shave and scrape
his fleeting terra-cotta vase
with hopes to form the perfect nape.

The anguish on the artist's face
is not perceived with art's embrace.
Its birth is not of much concern
when filling just the perfect space.

The Oz (a cyclical ruba'i)

There's nothing like the taste of wine
to make the afternoon divine,
a novel Main Street tasting room
gives townfolk pleasures of the vine.

The stress of life, the woe of whom
are waiting for the buds to bloom,
are leading to dysphoric blues,
yet wine may lift this hamlet's gloom.

The opening of Oz is news,
its storefront cast in vibrant hues,
their melancholy cast aside,
with cellar racks from which to choose.

The implications, county-wide,
is that the Oz will now provide
new wine selections never seen
in bergs once filled with civic pride.

The chefs now come with swank cuisine,
as Oz was in a magazine,
the town that once was in decline
is now the region's posh new scene.

Septolet

Like the musette, the septolet also has its roots in music. A "septulet" is a group of seven notes played in a certain way. From this a septolet has evolved to become a seven-line poem consisting of exactly fourteen words, constructed with two stanzas of three and four lines, in either order.

Like haiku, musettes, tanka, and other short forms, being poignant, rather than just clever, is ideal. But the septolet's two stanzas have another purpose, telling or describing two aspects of the same subject or scene, each reinforcing the other. Though the second stanza should not be a continuation of the first, it should still add to the reader's understanding of the subject at hand.

With such short lines, there is no meter. The title is at the poet's discretion, but can be used to enhance the septolet's point or theme.

Examples:

<u>Moving Day</u>

Three homes
to choose from,
all so
inviting.

The red
birdhouse-
that's my style!

Autumn Ivy

Ivy blankets
the north wall
in crimson and
orange.

It's been
green
long enough.

Sestina

One of the most challenging forms to master, the sestina is a very structured form of six sestets (six-line stanzas) followed by a triplet (or tercet, a three-line stanza) for a total of 39 lines. What sets it apart, however, is the re-use of the final word in each line of the first stanza in a specific order that is different in each subsequent stanza. All six repeating words appear in the triplet as well.

The sestet is usually strictly metered and is commonly written in decasyllables, or lines of ten syllables each, but other formal structures are acceptable. Rhyming is not a requirement of the form, but if the first stanza rhymes (i.e. a-b-c-a-b-c or a-b-a-b-a-b), the balance will rhyme by default, since the rhyming words are the ones repeated. However, the pattern of rhyme will only follow the sequence of last words for each stanza.

The notation for the last words is "1" through "6," for each of the six lines, thus the pattern of use is as follows:

Stanza 1: 1 2 3 4 5 6

Stanza 2: 6 1 5 2 4 3

Stanza 3: 3 6 4 1 2 5

Stanza 4: 5 3 2 6 1 4

Stanza 5: 4 5 1 3 6 2

Stanza 6: 2 4 6 5 3 1

Stanza 7: 6 2, 1 4, 5 3 (three lines)

The final triplet, using all six words in three lines, is a point in the sestet that can vary from form, using a different pattern (i.e. 1 2, 3 4, 5 6), or perhaps a couplet (two-line stanza, i.e. 6 2 1, 4 5 3). A rare format even ends on a haiku or senryu, utilizing the six repeated words in the accepted 5-7-5 syllabic pattern.

So, in the example below, 1=day, 2=cold, 3=place, 4=café, 5=hold and 6=embrace.

Examples:

<u>A Picturesque Café</u>

Regardless of the time of day,
or if a tempest's rain is cold,
my mind will wander to the place
where first we met, that quaint café,
when both our lives were still on hold;
we hadn't had our first embrace.

The world had left me to embrace
a job I suffered through each day,
no inspiration taking hold,
relentless as a common cold.
But in this picturesque café
my life was never out of place.

I hadn't known that in this place
I'd found a reason to embrace
my future and this old café.
I made my mind up on this day
that though the season's turning cold,
the promise of its warmth I'd hold.

A notion started, keeping hold,
that there was something in this place
which bore the brunt of passions cold,
where many felt love's kind embrace,
escaping from their trying day--
I'd someday own this aged café.

The atmosphere of my café,
an ambiance of which would hold
the patrons' kindness through the day-
this would be the only place
to offer all a warm embrace,
a lively shelter from the cold.

Through summer's drought and winter's cold,
my friends would come to my café
to help each other, love, embrace
camaraderie, while couples hold
each other, like no other place
to spend their lives day after day.

I longingly embrace the cold
and greet the day in our cafe,
take hold of this, our perfect place.

The Cure

Horizons from his tower room
reach out beyond the city's brink.
the urban squall would not allow
a focused mind that yearns to think.
This lonely room with lab arrays
implores to find the missing link.

His formal cuff and shiny link,
a tie that leaves so little room
to breathe, while food in deft arrays
catch eyes of guests, so near the brink,
those glasses filled, he starts to think
that this is all he can allow.

The money men would still allow
these moments and his tepid link,
the public never poised to think
that posturing in cluttered room
is science, nearly on the brink
of finding cures in drug arrays.

As newsmen focus on arrays
of solar panels, they allow
enthusiasm's thinning brink
to bubble forth, though never link
the scientist to battle room,
yet still his mind is forced to think.

Distractions bring no time to think
of colored pathogen arrays,
no time to give those bugs the room
to grow as antidotes allow.
The scientist removed the link,
rolled up his cuff, approached the brink.

And just before he reached the brink
of setback, he had dared to think
that culture six, a broken link
of growth, among those glass arrays,
would be the one that would allow
success to fill that tower room.

The deadened link had breached the brink
of failure, leaving most to think
what new arrays of medicines allow.

Sijo

The sijo is an ancient form of Korean poetry that often employs pastoral (related to a shepherd's nomadic lifestyle in the countryside), metaphysical or cosmological themes, though others subjects are allowed. A classic sijo consists of three lines of 14 to 16 syllables each, for a total of 44 to 46 syllables. Some modern poets have begun to split these lines in half to make the poem a sestet (6 lines), keeping the syllable count. A sijo is normally narrative, without rhyming or meter.

Similar to a sonnet, a sijo may introduce a situation (in its first line), a development (in line two), and a conclusion or twist. However, a sijo's conclusion is seldom witty. Like haiku, sijo may include metaphors, puns, or symbolic word play.

The name is left to the poet's discretion, but is usually taken from a word or phrase within the poem.

Examples:

<u>I See No Anger</u>

I see no anger in the sky, just an artistic rendition,
a child's jigsaw puzzle of cobalt blue, white and ominous gray.
Rather, I count my blessings in an endless celestial palette.

<u>Geometric Domes</u>

Elegant beauty of geometry hides in plain sight.
Architects can only dream of such vogue appreciation.
Tourists crane their necks gawking at unexpected works of art.

Sonnet

One of my favorite poetic forms, a sonnet consists of fourteen lines and can have different stanza groupings and rhyming patterns, depending on the style preferred. Sonnets usually have a "turn" or conclusion, whereby a problem or scenario begins to be rectified or explained. I have written about fifty sonnets, including English, Spenserian and Italian styles.

Though sometimes written in a single 14-line stanza, a classic English sonnet contains three quatrains (four lines each) and a couplet (two lines), is written in iambic tetrameter or pentameter (four or five iterations of "dah-DUM" in a line), and has the rhyming pattern:

a-b-a-b ... c-d-c-d ... e-f-e-f ... g-g

Similarly, a Spenserian sonnet uses a rhyming scheme of:

a-b-a-b ... b-c-b-c ... c-d-c-d ... e-e

An Italian sonnet may vary widely in pattern, but usually consists of two quatrains (or an 8-line "octet") followed by a sestet (six lines), and rhymes:

a-b-b-a ... a-b-b-a ... c-d-c-d-c-d

Other meters may be used for sonnets, such as anapestic (see the "Poetic Meter" chapter) or even prose, which is unmetered and unrhymed. Consistency and flow is the key, leading to the turn or conclusion. I have a special affinity for sonnets because, like haiku, you can emphasize or drive home a point, but you get more than a line or two to do so.

Here are some examples.

The following is an English sonnet:

The World Is There

The drab and bleak existence set aside,
my corner of the neighborhood, secured,
to go beyond would fight the rising tide
of factions gathered, waiting for the lured.

I shuffle by on paths of comfort, eased,
to work assignments sheltered from the hoards,
and home again, without a moment seized
to recognize the richness life affords.

Sometimes our spirit shakes itself to find
that status quo and safety can't replace
enrichment of the soul, still intertwined
with nature and its awe-inspired grace.

The world is there for humans to behold
and interact as spectacles unfold.

This is a Spenserian sonnet:

The Heron

The heron flies with neck retracted, short,
unlike its friend, the long-necked, graceful swan,
and though they're known by egret, also sport
the moniker of bittern, now foregone.

No easy life, these water fowl dwell on,
with fish entrapped when fortunate to dine.
They nest, find marshy ground to build upon
or teeter on a branch with keen design.

The "lady of the waters" in decline
as wetlands shrink from man's intruding use,
the heron is oblivious to signs
of human disregard and land abuse.

They stalk their prey and stab with sharpened beak
while unaware of avian mystique.

Lastly, an Italian sonnet:

Riverboat Gambler

The gambler leaned across the aisle
and tucked the sleeve of Miss Louise.
"Excuse the interruption, please,
do we have time to play a while?"

The callow Miss held back a smile,
for now she didn't want to tease.
"Why, sir, I think there's time to squeeze
a game or two, if that's worthwhile."

She found him in the poker room
much later, leaving with the pot.
"Now, boys," he said, "please don't assume
my winning here is luck, it's not.
Just skill, I promise, I presumed
that cheating here would get me shot."

Standard Habbie

The "standard Habbie" has also been called the Scottish Stanza, the Burns Stanza (after Robert Burns, widely known as the national poet of Scotland), or the six-line stave. This form was named for Habbie Simpson, who was a poet and the town piper of the Scottish village of Kilbarchan in the sixteenth century. Interestingly, Habbie didn't invent the form named for him. Instead, he was the subject of the first known poem in this format, "The Life and death of Habbie Simpson," written by Robert Sempill the younger of Beltrees in 1640.

Initially strictly lyrical, often the standard Habbie is comical or satirical. It can also be used to describe an interesting aspect of life or to give a picture of the times.

The standard Habbie is written in any number of six-line stanzas. In each stanza, lines 1,2,3 and 5 use four metrical feet and rhyme with each other, while lines 4 and 6 use two feet and rhyme with each other. A metrical foot is a small segment of syllables, such as "dah-DUM" or "dah-dah-DUM" (see the "Poetic Meter" chapter), that are repeated in a line or stanza to form a pattern.

The following show the line, rhyming notation and number of feet through two stanzas of the standard Habbie:

L1- a -4-feet	L7- c -4-feet
L2- a -4-feet	L8- c -4-feet
L3- a -4-feet	L9- c -4-feet
L4- b -2-feet	L10- d -2-feet
L5- a -4-feet	L11- c -4-feet
L6- b -2-feet	L12- d -2-feet

A variation of the Habbie uses seven-line stanzas with the pattern a-a-b-c-c-b (the "b" lines are the shortened ones). There are no rules on naming.

Examples:

<u>My Summer Placation</u>

The months of work, my project done,
the big account at long last won,
my wife resolved we'd have some fun,
like she had dreamed.
Before it even had begun,
I kicked and screamed

The last thing on my burdened mind
was flying in a plane, confined;
while tasks were getting more behind,
I wouldn't rest.
But though I madly fussed and whined,
I acquiesced.

Surprised, I did relax one day,
engaged in monuments to play,
concerns lost in a Greek soiree,
I was reposed,
the Eiffel replica's cafe
was never closed.

The firm endured without me there,
my ego checked, I'm now aware
that workaholics can repair
their one-track lives.
A foliage outing we'll prepare
as Fall arrives.

Harboring Prose

With one look they can change people's woeful despair
with their oversized petals of gold, unaware
of attention they garner with impassive flair
by the odd passers-by,
a hushed whisper of wind gently sweeps without care,
as if nothing's awry.

As the sun tracks the sky, it is followed by those
pretty sunflower faces, together they pose
in a field of poetry harboring prose,
and if only they could,
they'd uncover their stalks and set out for, who knows?
without limits, for good!

Tanka

Originating in ancient Japan, a tanka (ton'- kah;) consisted of a haiku sent by mail or messenger and a two-line reply added to it for the returned message. Now tanka are composed in their final, familiar five-line format.

You may recall that haiku does not rhyme and consists of 17 syllables in three lines in a 5–7–5 format (five syllables in line one, seven in line two, then five again). A tanka adds two unrhymed lines of seven syllables each, for a total of 31 syllables. It can be in the 5-7-5-7-7 or in the two-stanza 5-7-5 ... 7-7 format.

Since they are short, titles of tanka may be taken from the poem's first line or a key line, or are simply numbered, though naming poems is completely up to the author without specific rules.

Examples:

A Summer Sail

A cool, windswept sea
and unassuming sunshine
reveal in silence
my lust for a summer sail,
emplacing my true bearing.

Weather Vanes

On a lonely road
I spy odd metal sculptures.
It's obvious now-

Old farmers pass and become
weather vanes on rolling plains.

Midweek Marina

Midweek marina,
your sails long for open sea.
While naked masts point
upward to the Wednesday sky,
sailors are anchored to desks.

Terza Rima

The terza rima was originated by the Italian poet Dante (1265-1321) in the Middle Ages, followed in use by such masters as Milton, Shelley and Byron. Many modern poets have also thrived with the form, such as Robert Frost and T.S. Eliot.

A terza rima is a series of triplets (3-line stanzas) with an interlocking rhyming scheme, ending in a single line or couplet. There is no limit to the number of triplets, and usually iambic pentameter (see the "Poetic Meter" chapter) is employed, though other classic meters are sometimes used. The rhyming pattern is connects each stanza to the following one:

a-b-a ... b-c-b ... c-d-c ... d-e-d ... e-e

There are no naming conventions for the terza rima.

Examples:

<u>The Keeper of the Grounds</u>

Just yesterday he made giraffes,
a dragonfly and circus clowns;
he loves the way each tourist laughs.

The clever keeper of the grounds
creates his topiary art;
a lifetime here, he still astounds.

Today his cannons will impart
reminders of the battles past,
of conquests made with grit and heart.

His garden actors will be cast
in parts portrayed in pinks and greens
by shrubs and flora holding fast.

One walks along organic scenes-
imagination intervenes.

Horizon Beckons

The rigging set and baggage loaded aft,
I point the bow into the western gust,
as I, alone, will guide this sailing craft.

Horizon beckons, wind provides the thrust,
the double masts are leaning slightly port,
and cutting through the whitecaps is a must.

I think about this trip, a last resort,
and watch as shoreline features saunter by,
still thankful for my family's support.

The rat race slowly fading with a sigh,
I pray my practice runs had been enough,
and judge the risk of tempests in July.

My focus changes as the sea gets rough,
I drop the canvas sails to fix the sway,
and drift back to the overhanging bluff.

Tonight, like others in a placid bay,
is healing to my mind and aching back.
Secluded, I enjoy a cabernet.

As days go by, I keep the boat on track,
my destination close, the end is near,
I've made up for adventure that I've lacked.

My jaunt into the nautical frontier
has given me the strength that I'll revere.

Trilinea

Research on the Trilinea form has left me scratching my head. I have found a few websites where poets have posted some verses in that genre, but no sites that describe them or their history. It is not a classical form, from what I can gather, so it was invented by a contemporary writer, but whom that was is a mystery still to be unraveled.

I do know the format, however, and it is short and sweet. Similar to haiku, the trilinea consists of three unrhymed lines, leading me to believe that haiku was its basis. Its syllable count is slightly different at 4-8-4, for a total of sixteen. One large caveat: the word "rose" must be placed within the poem.

Other than that, I can find no other requirements, so theme and title are at the poet's discretion; though including "rose" may dictate the subject somewhat. I have seen the word used as a color, a flower, an action and even a name, as well as the plural form, so evidently one can be quite creative in following this rule.

Here are my examples:

Exuberance

Free from scissors
and indoor vase, wild roses bare
exuberance!

Optimism

My rose-colored
mind prevents me from seeing you
as bad for me.

Triolet

The form stems from medieval French poetry; the earliest known examples are from the late 13th century.

The Triolet is an eight-line form, usually in iambic tetrameter or pentameter (see the "Poetic Meter" chapter), that uses two refrains. A refrain is a line that is repeated one or more times in a poem. Line 1 repeats as lines 4 and 7, and line 2 as the last line. Therefore, the first two lines are repeated as the last two lines.

There is some flexibility in the refrains, and it is traditional to use two halves of at least one of the refrains in different contexts, which I try to do. The format is as follows (line-rhyme or line-refrain):

L1- a
L2- b
L3- a
L4- refrain (L1)
L5- a
L6- b
L7- refrain (L1)
L8- refrain (L2)

Like most poetic forms we've been discussing, the title is completely up to the poet.

Examples:

Passage Rites

I grew up fast, I missed my dad's advice,
and I was forced to skip the passage rites.
The oldest of the kids, I paid the price
and grew up fast. I longed for dad's advice,
adulthood seemed so daunting, so concise-
no boyhood dreams, no bugs beneath the lights.
I grew up fast while missing Dad's advice
when I was forced to skip the passage rites.

Dusk on the Delta

The dim of dusk calms delta's shoal,
and soon begins cacophony,
its tenants anxious to patrol.
The dim of dusk calms delta's shoal,
the feral night would soon console
nocturnal beasts' disharmony.
The dim of dusk calms delta's shoal,
and soon begins cacophony.

Villanelle

Though its name sounds French and has its roots in the Medieval Europe, most villanelles have been written in English. This form is thought to have come from Spanish or Italian ballad-like folk songs, without any strict format or length. The villanelle's current structure wasn't widely used until the nineteenth century when the form was made popular by author Theodore de Banville. Probably the most famous villanelle is the classic poem by Dylan Thomas, "Do Not Go Gentle into that Good Night."

A villanelle is nineteen lines long, consisting of five tercets (three-line stanzas) and one concluding quatrain (four line stanza), with only two rhyme sounds. The first and third lines of the first stanza are rhyming refrains that alternate as the third line in each successive stanza and form a couplet at the close.   A refrain is a line that repeats one or more times in a poem.

A notation for this scheme might look like this:

L1- a refrain(1)
L2- b
L3- a refrain(2)

L4- a
L5- b
L6- a refrain(1)

L7- a
L8- b
L9- a refrain(2)

L10- a
L11- b
L12- a refrain(1)

L13- a
L14- b
L15- a refrain(2)

L16- a
L17- b
L18- a refrain(1)
L19- a refrain(2)

In this notation "refrain(1)" refers to repeating line 1 and "refrain(2)" means repeating line 2.

In developing a villanelle, many poets start by writing the two rhyming refrains first, keeping in mind that the lines are more interesting if they can be taken in different context with each use, and then fill in the other lines. This way eight of the nineteen lines are complete immediately. You may name a villanelle as you please.

Examples:

<u>The Crowded Square</u>

The rabble in the crowded square
had waited for their lord to speak
to bring them from their deep despair.

His majesty was well aware
that enemies abroad would seek
the rabble in the crowded square.

The lord appeared, so debonair,
and cheers became a growing pique
to bring them from their deep despair.

The beggars jeered the staid affair,
and soon they joined with harsh critique
the rabble in the crowded square.

The lord began his evening prayer
and pleaded, commerce was so bleak,
to bring them from their deep despair.

And then the lord removed his stare,
and asked, with sober, blushing cheek,
the rabble in the crowded square
to bring them from their deep despair.

The Tourist

He shoots his camera with a postured stare,
his targets, an indigenous soiree,
to fill the online scrapbook he'd prepare.

Though shirtless in this hot and muggy air,
his attitude depicts a grand cliche-
he shoots his camera with a postured stare,

With trinkets bought inside the market square,
he'll buy more souvenirs and put away
to fill the online scrapbook he'd prepare.

With treks providing views beyond compare,
of tropical locale and sleepy bay,
he shoots his camera with a postured stare,

The Caribbean mood, with vivid flair,
would give him snapshots of the locals' play
to fill the online scrapbook he'd prepare.

The tourist wanders, mostly unaware
that those around will grin at the display,
he shoots his camera with a postured stare,
to fill the online scrapbook he'd prepare.

Virelai

The virelai is a type of French lyric poetry written in the Middle Ages by troubadours and was one of the most popular forms set to music in Medieval Europe. However, there has been some conjecture that it was not invented by the French as it is similar to lyric verse in other European cultures of the 14th, 15th and 16th centuries. Examples would be the English carol, the Arabic muwashshaḥ, the Italian lauda and frottola, and the Spanish villancico.

The virelai consists of at least two stanzas of three "lais" each. A lai is a tercet (three-line segment) of 5, 5 and 2 syllables which rhyme "a-a-b." Therefore, each nine-line stanza has syllable counts of:

5-5-2-5-5-2-5-5-2

and a rhyming pattern of:

a-a-b-a-a-b-a-a-b

Another wrinkle is that the rhyme from the short lines of one stanza continue as the rhyme of the long lines of the next. The short lines of the last stanza then rhyme with the long lines of the first, making the cyclical rhyme complete. A three-stanza pattern would be:

a-a-b-a-a-b-a-a-b ... b-b-c-b-b-c-b-b-c ... c-c-a-c-c-a-c-c-a

There are no naming guidelines in the virelai.

Example:

The Rivershore Lighthouse

The lighthouse is there,
as riverboats share
the night
with those unaware
of thick, murky air,
the blight
of captains who stare
into fog, and swear
in fright.

A bright beam of white,
dark changes to light
this eve,
fear turns to delight.
With shorelines in sight,
they weave
their pattern and fight
to tack left and right,
to leave.

Now no need to grieve,
the lighthouse achieves
this prayer,
the skippers perceive
their safety, relieved
and spared-
no injured, bereaved,
no ships to receive
repair.

Wave Poem

A wave poem utilizes increasing and decreasing syllable counts to resemble a series of ocean swells. There are a variety of "shape" formats in poetry, whereby a poet uses the words and spaces to draw a particular shape or visual pattern, such as a Chinese lantern, a tree, or a flower. The wave simulates a series of ocean waves.

Usually consisting of short lines of less than eight syllables, the theme and pattern sets a soothing tone, describing scenes of nature, climate, sunsets, sailing, or other display of tranquility.

As with most poetry utilizing syllable patterns, such as haiku, tanka or etherees, meter and rhyme are not utilized.

In my research, one form description suggested a syllable pattern of:

1, 2, 1, 2, 3, 2, 1, 2, 3, 4, 3, 2, 1, 2, 3, 2, 1, 2, 1

but this is not the only pattern available. It should have at least three "waves" however to ensure the soothing pattern, such as:

1, 2, 3, 4, 3, 2, 1, 2, 3, 4, 3, 2, 1, 2, 3, 4, 3, 2, 1

There are no guidelines for titling a wave poem, so it is author's choice.

Example:

The Blanket

Fall,
in full
spectacle,
oranges, golds,
flaming reds,
once green,
calls
to those
who listen,
so patiently
painting leaves
before the
winter
comes.
Sadly,
very soon
the brisk north wind
will tear the
brilliant
shades
from limbs
grudgingly
surrendering
their blanket
to the
cold.

Epilogue

There are new and remarkable poetic forms being invented almost continually in the literary world, and I have only described here the classic forms and the interesting formats I've discovered along my own writing path. I tend toward rhyming poetry in an iambic meter, sort of my own "top dead center," as my dad used to say. Recognizing this, I strive to wander left and right, challenging my own comfort and ease as often as I am able.

I am a true believer in thoroughly mastering rules before you purposely break them. Once practiced, don't be afraid to experiment in meter and rhyming patterns, stanza breaks and refrains, or other conventions.

Bad poetry is everywhere, especially with the Internet giving so many people a pulpit. There are things you can do and things to avoid to keep from becoming one of the unpoetic masses.

First, join a poetry site that thrives on critique and grow a thick skin. Read many of the comments and see if you agree with the assessments and suggestions. I like GotPoetry.com because of the quality of active members there, but dozens of similar communities exist.

Second, learn how to rhyme in such a way that the rhymes are more natural speech than those forced into a line for the expressed purpose of rhyming. Reading the masters will clue you in on what great rhyme is like. There are many good rhyming dictionaries on line, and they can give you rhymes that may fit in a line well that you never thought of.

Much of my time writing poetry is spent on trying to make rhymes feel natural in their context, employing words or phrases that are not used purely for their rhymes. People don't speak in rhymes, so reading forced rhymes can be a big distraction. You want the rhyme to be matter-of-fact, letting people read the feeling or purpose of the word rather than focus on the rhyme. This can be difficult, and I don't always accomplish it, but I strive for that type of perfection in my poetry nonetheless.

Next, don't pour out your thoughts and feelings into your work. Instead, be poignant, be interesting, be insightful. It's the poet's duty to be profound. Calculate the effect the right words will have upon the reader.

Avoid clichés. Leave over-used phrases and worn-out clichés to lyricists and song writers. For fun, I just Googled "lyrics I still love you" and got 53,900,000 results, literally. Do you really want to say the same thing, the same way, as thousands of other poets through the ages? Find a way to make a theme uniquely yours.

Last, write often. How do you get to Carnegie Hall? Practice!

About the Author

Jack Huber has long been a writer of technical articles, having been published in both print and online periodicals, newsletters and portals. He had his first poems published at age ten when his fifth grade teacher submitted two pieces that were accepted by a literary magazine. Since then Jack has written poetry off and on throughout his life, as well as taking thousands of pictures as photo buff. His love of photography and interest in poetry were finally combined with his fondness of exploring America for his growing body of work.

 Jack currently lives in Wichita, Kansas. In addition to writing and photography, Jack enjoys wine, travel, and singing karaoke.

His books of poetry and photographs include "Aspects Long Forgotten," "A Splendid Alternative," "A Troupe In Masquerade," "Trappings of the Years," and "An Eerie Calm Before the Night."

For more information, go to *http://www.jackhuber.com*.